Bitter&Sweet

A mixture of emotions

Prisha Goel

BookLeaf Publishing

India | USA | UK

Made with ❤ on the BookLeaf Publishing Platform
www.bookleafpub.in
www.bookleafpub.com

Dedication

For the words you never heard
and the words you never said.

Preface

I am writing this poetry book in order to support others who have been through traumatic experiences in their life and tell them that they are not alone. I pour my heart out in it like what I went, how I felt throughout my life about various things, that trauma I went throughout my life till now. I just gave them a voice, a way to let them out and a way to connect with you all. As a member of the LGBTQ+ community, I'm here to support them, to tell people that we exist and we are valid and we can achieve the same things as cis and heterosexual people. I'm here to inspire all the writers out there whether they are a member of the community or not, don't stop! Believe in yourself and just grow more and more.

Acknowledgements

I want to thank my friends for encouraging me, always giving honest feedback of my poems and pushing me more to improve, more to write and never give up. Thanks to the artist I adore for providing me comfort, providing me a will to live and providing me something to hold onto. If it wasn't for them, I might not have been alive by now and writing this book.

Thanks to my parents for supporting me and standing with me in this, for giving me this golden opportunity to present my work to the world and special mention to my friend Vaanya who worked tooth and nail in order to get me out of my writing block.

At last, I want to thank my readers who made it this far and are giving me more motivation I'm glad to have you all.

1. Blessing or a curse?

She had a beautiful face
Always the first in every race
She aced in studies
She was a fun loving girl with no worries
Her lover was her moon
Who became the light in the dark
And made her shine in every part
Everything was perfect
Her life was the best
She was roaming and enjoying with her friends
Suddenly someone on the bike
Threw something on her
Now there's vicious acid on her face
Face started burning
Eyes started blurring
World felt like it's ending
Those fragile, weak men fled
Now she is on the hospital bed
Thinking about the day she said "No I'm sorry"
He was mesmerised by her face
She didn't want to date
Now the unwanted, meaningless regret
Took its shape
Covering her

Swallowing her
Standing near the bathroom sink
Thinking
How everything changed in a blink
She thought about that lovely, charming girl
She thought about that face
Then she cried
And said
"GOD, why, why did you write this down in my fate?"
In her eyes, that beautiful face was just a Phase
But oh god, someone tell
Her she looks
Beautiful in
Every
Single
Way
A blessing turned into a curse
Oh lord! Let them burn first
A blessing turned into a curse
Oh lord! Let them burn first
A blessing turned into a curse...

2. Demise

A gloomy night
The day of demise
Filled with grief, filled with cries
Mournful people
The place I called 'home' is gone forever now
It hurts like a needle
An ocean overflowing with emotions,
With emptiness
I wish I could go back in time and tell him
How much I love him
How much he meant to me
How thankful I am to have him
How I admire him
It felt like a wire was cut from the socket
And the socket is now
Useless,
Flawed...
I am the socket,
Now my night is moonless
"Who was he?" You may question
He was a maude
A Mighty in battle
Someone who was fearless
Someone who loved her like Achilles had loved

Patroclus
Someone who was filled with sacrifices
he was filled with lies too
Because
He promised me he will never leave me
Still he did
He left me alone
All alone in this world full of judgments
Full of fake commitments
He loved every part of me
"Who was he?" You ask
He was the tree of my treehouse
He was my home
I believe I may have said this earlier
But I am saying it now
I love you unconditionally.

To him who becomes moonlight to save my dark night

3. Apricity

Your love gives warmth like blankets give in winter
Feeling you is like a cold breeze, always comforting,
Oh lord, what magic did she do on me
When I close my eyes, I see her
There standing and god
She is impeccable
 irreplaceable
If you ever read this and don't believe me
My love,
Ask my pillow
How I hug it everyday imagining your arms around me
How I hold it
Gently with warmth like leaves falling down from trees
in fall
Ask my blanket
That's how I kick my feet while talking to you
Ask my room's wall
How I rehearse proposing to you, how I talk about you
with my friends
How do I describe you?
 ask my walls
ask my mirror, how my face lights up, how all the
tension from my face eases up
And lastly

Ask how brightly I smile when I think about you, how I
cry when we fight
But darling, you are my warmth in cold
You are my
Aprictiy.

~yours truly

4. Where's my home

I don't belong here
This lingering feeling
Peeling my skin
Cutting my parts
Breaking every bone
Giving up all of them one by one
Screaming.
Crying.
Throwing.
They all say "I'm here" but they are really not
A knot in the chest
Thoughts in mind
Thinking when will this misery end
Meanwhile my body rots
It's like a slippery floor no matter how much you try I
always fall
I try reaching out, there's no one to hold on to
Blood runs cold
Breath starts getting heavier
Things get scarier
loneliness in me starts to grow and grow
The more it grows the more I throw
 my parts away
I never let other person know

But they always betray
I still stay, in a hope of someday they'll come around
They don't.
I see those stories and cry
I try to stay positive
But it gets negative
I write just to not write anything
I keep editing the words so they can fit within my
'friends' style
So they keep talking to me
Changed myself into a person that I hate
The parts I cut I sell them and the rate is a friend
Yes, friends aren't bought but earned
But
I want to know the feeling of having friends even if they
just pretend
Just once I want to know how it feels to have someone
I try to talk just to be told to shut up
"You, need to learn how to enjoy your own company"
but till when?
Why am I not enough?
All these questions in my mind
Answers are nowhere to be found
It's tiring
Someone just pretend to be my friend
I'm dying.

~loneliness inside me

5. Him

And my heartbeat drops
Stomach starts sinking in
Guilt swallowing me
The need of him to be here taking over
Its like a hangover
A hangover which has no end
No matter how much I try to blend with other people
At last, he is the one I yearn for him
Everything was perfect but it took a turn
Why?
Those bridges we both built
To meet at
Burned down
And I cant do anything about it
Anything but yearn...
Regret...
Cry...
No matter how much I try to forget
It always comes back
All my tries to move on
Goes into drain
And all I'm left with, is...
Pain
Pain, so hurtful, so terrible, so

Horrific,
Intolerable
Yet I have to tolerate it
I just suffer everyday
Someone close my mind's
Shutter
A lot to say yet I don't
Utter a word
Its a hustle yet,
All I can do is
Suffer...
Just suffer.

~someone living with pain, dying like there's poison in
their viens

6. Feelings

This feeling...
This feeling is strange.
 I never felt it before...
It's something new out of my range
This nervousness is tearing me apart
Consuming every part
And
now it's cutting my bones and flesh
The wounds are fresh.
The feeling of being alone is old
Bring the food on the plate of gold
And I still wouldn't eat
I don't want to.
Or do I?
It doesn't matter
So what matters is my size
But I'm tired
I can't eat.
I can't sleep.
I can't even stand on my feet...

~written by people who are in cage filled with rage

7. Reminders of him

While reading a book
I get reminders for him
A tear escapes from my eyes
"The softness his hands carry... they just melt like a
butter and we become one"
This line gave me a reminder of him
Of that day in rain
Where his soft hands landed on my bare waist
We danced, we laughed, we kissed
And walked home together
Because we missed the train
"You are in my brain, in my mind, you... You are the one
who makes my world shine"
"Shine"
 Thiis word gave me a reminder of his coffee pigmented
eyes
They shone the best and made me shine
From, south to north, east to west
All over the world
Now his smell is pervaded in my veins
But he is gone
I'll always remember him
In my memory lane...

8. Cherries

The taste of your lips is like cherries...
My favourite.
We built myriads of our love
Filled with petals of the roses you gave me...
Filled with warmth
We sat under the stars
admiring each other
I loved when we held our hands
The way our hands locked
Sun compliments your brown eyes
They shine the best
Your eyes, face, your hands, your skin...
You were beautiful, adored by me in
Every single way...
We loved each other like a sky
Infinite...

But then why did we throw it away?
Why did those stars start to fade?
Why did our kiss turned into fury?
The hands we held were holding together

Became agony
We danced under rain
We played with flowers in the spring
We sat together under a tree in autumn
Gave each other a damaged leaf
And said that...
"We would love each other even if few parts were
missing...
We would fly in the air together
And then finally we rest and will find peace together"
Cherries will be my favourite forever...

9. The magical touch

And the kiss was gentle...
So gentle like petals...
Full of passion just like an artist filled with passion for
the art
Filled with tenderness
Filled with love
It wasn't a kiss
It was the promise he made to her
Promise of giving her moon to stars
Promise that he would cut parts of himself to fill hers
He will drink poison pretending it's amrit
If given by her
The man who never bowed to any man
He bowed to her
He would go on his knees,
He would tear the worlds apart
Even the world he made for himself
Just for her...

~Someone who will bring down the stars and moon for
her

10. A lonley heart

This rope is named loneliness. Wrapped around my neck,
Everyday it's just waiting for me hang on it
I find ways to cope but I find none
Not even a single one
It's so simple how people say "Let it go."
Like it didn't cripple your heart
Like it didn't shatter your heart
Like it didn't leave a scar on your mind
I scribble words and words just to find answers
But all I find is more questions
"Try finding distractions" they say but how?
How can I sit and do other things and not think
Every blink turns into tears
Every drink I drink turns into poison
Every noise turns into the words that I can't handle
Every thing I eat turns into a knot in my chest due to
which I can't breathe
The rope is choking harder
The more I live the more the end of this misery gets
farther
Farther above in the sky that I can't reach...

I see them happy without me and I'm happy for them but

What happened to the promises we made?
The plans we made?
The memories we made?
Im fading, I'm dying
I scream but no one listens
Their actions creeps inside me
Making me bleed...
More... And more...
I search the street but found no one
Now it's a long street with no one around
I ring the bell
No one answers
My thoughts killing me from inside
My eyes weep my mouth shake
My mind freeze
Rope around my throat chokes me harder and harder
I'm dying...

11. Love

Love is tender, pure, warm...
Warm like a hug in icy weather...
It is meant to be held with gentleness...
Its meant to be filled by kindness...
Love is something we always give...
To everyone, but ourselves..
Why?
Your body is distinctive. Something only you can carry
Your strech marks are like rivers of valley
The way river flows in curves With rocks in between
them
Your eyes are like gems
Shining brighter and brighter
The more I look into them...
The softer they get...
Your face is filled with grace.
Your smile makes my day.
Your magnificent voice .
Rejoice!
Your hair for me is like melted butter...
Whenever I see you it makes my heart flutter...

12. Emptiness

There's an emptiness inside
I may look fine but I'm numb
Those autumn leaves don't comfort me anymore...
Those sound tips of rain don't make me wanna dance
anymore...
That amazing smell of custard doesn't crave me
anymore...
Those long calls with friends don't make me smile
anymore...
Those hang outs with friends are like lost somewhere I
don't feel the happiness
That slap of my mother doesn't bother me anymore...
I don't cry.
I just go to my room and sleep
Not being able to spend time with papa doesn't annoy
me anymore
I just watch reels
That slowly drifting away relationship
Doesn't make me panic anymore...
What affects me? Nothing.
I'm a statue with a heart of gold..
Who is tired of waiting for the person who would kiss
me and bring me back to life
I'm a pillow cover...

Always thrown away
Waiting for somebody to pick up
But
The fact I gotta do everything on my own
 I need to be the person who brings me back to life
I need to force myself to be so perfect that no one can
throw me away
I need to suck the nectar out of my flower in order to live
just like a butterfly
I know I
Can
Do
This
Own my own
I've got me but this me is leaving the body
Making me feel empty numb
This is a letter to emptiness telling that I'm undefeated...

"You can let it go you can throw a party to everyone you
know" (harry styles)

(C'est la vie)

13. Loneliness

Empty head..
Empty bottles..
Puddle of tears..
Losing everything we fear
Loud cries
No one to hear
I will accept even bare
But there's no one here
I miss those games of truth and dare..
Where the smiles were real, now they are rare...
Their names echo in my head
Some are scattered...
And
Some are dead...
I see people smiling bright
And enjoying the whole day and night
I'm happy for them but
But oh! The jealousy...
I wish I had someone
Whose voice is melody to my ears,
Those laughs,
Those long walks,
Those long talks,

Without worrying about time and not seeing the
watches
And the feeling of knowing
If you'll fall there's always
Someone to hold
I'm not bold enough to talk
Or it's been so long that I forgot how to talk
Always craving that interaction
But I go cold whenever it's time to act
I've tried every method of distraction
But at the end
I only meet me and my depression
Hundreds body in graveyard
And I buried myself so far
That one can ever reach
Hundred feet into the ground
You will find a golden heart filled with wounds,
I know it might sound dramatic to you
But it's traumatic
I observe those eye smiles when
A girl meets her sister
I observe the high-fives
When two bros meet each other
And it hurts
When I see that shy smile on a girl's face
When he flirts
It's just me and my cuts

Not enough that one can keep
Not pretty enough one can date
But shitty enough that someone uses me and discards me
away
I guess this is my fate...

~a person with a golden heart

14. Proud?

Can't be too loud...
Can't be too proud...
I can't be too proud...
Can't be loud...
People leave
Memory stays
People leave
Memory stays
And it weaves a cloud full of thoughts
Feeling broken...
Stuck in those words which are unspoken...
Open wounds...
Loud sounds...
Of people saying negative things
About me
I'm so lost
Someone find me..
Hold me gently...
Not let go of me
Not even slightly
I see other people of my age Shining so brightly and
doing things like a piece of cake
Are they fake? I ask myself daily...
This is not a poem...

These are my feelings...
If I go directly to the point
Don't wanna live...
Don't wanna exist...
Just leave...

~thoughts of someone's mind

15. Why?

Why did you leave?
Why didn't you try to stop me?
You just said alright...
That's all..
I gave you my whole
And you threw me into the dark hole
Now someone seize this pain Give me peace again
"Sucide... suicide..." echoes in my head
But what's the point of suicide?
It's a homicide
I fell in love
All because of the time and distance
I still stare at the text "alright"
You didn't even try...
I'm too numb to cry
It's too hard to say goodbye...
Why?
Why my love why did you leave?
"Why..." echos in my head
And I try... And try...
To forget you...
It's been days without you and I'm already feeling that...
Emptiness...

My friends are witnesses
What you did to me is cruel but I can't hate you after
you got sweet soul
I will neither hate you...
Nor I'll love anyone like I love you...

16. Missing from you

I am missing from you

That gorgeous smile
Those sweet talks
That secret file
dedicated to you
Those mindlessly wandering thoughts...
Those scattered feelings...
Those blissful eyes...
And
Our souls are tied
Those freshly plucked flowers and...
Your laughter growing louder
That one little kiss and
I make a fist that nervousness rising
And that little chuckle and words "next date I'm deciding
"

The fear that never leaves
Those eyes I never want to weep
Those kisses, those laughters, that holding hands those
beautiful moments I want to keep
That walking on the vehicles side
Those men I would put up a fight
For you

That hidden yet not so hidden love
Those goodbyes that I want to forbidden and forgotten
Those teary eyes of mine
When you said
Yes.
A scream leaves my body
Tho the fear of losing another person I love creeps my
soul
I put it aside
Those issues of me missing you way too much
that loss of time but I only search for where is that
Person that I call
Mine.
I am missing from you
A piece of me is missing from me
That fondness of cats
And the scream you leave when you see a rat
These pieces are missing from me
Those three words
I love you
Are sweetest
Oh baby I would take a bullet for you
I would shoot a bullet for you
Everything illegal seems legal when it's for you
I am missing from you

~to those who are missing from me

17. A question Never can be answered

A question never can be answered: why did you leave?

I stare at the text "alright"
You didn't even tried to stop me why
You came like a wind left like breeze
Someone seize this pain and give me peace again
You were my mirbane to the perfume
Without you I'm nothing
Now I'm shutting down again
My all efforts went in vain
I'm the one to blame
Because I broke up and you said just alright
Homicide
And you were quite right "we won't work"
And here I still believed
You are at ease and I'm the one saying please, please
someone save me from the darkness
You were key to my home
Now there's no home no key
Only me and my red eyes
You never asked me to be psych
I am still staring at the text "alright"
Oh my dear! You came like wind left like a breeze

You texted me rarely
You didn't miss me
You lost me
I gave you my all
And you threw it into the bin
You win you win this fight
And you fell first just by seeing my brown eyes full of
joy
Now I hate those eyes hate that green dress by which
you were impressed
I'm too numb to cry...
Too numb to feel anything but emptiness
Oh my dear love... why did you leave so easily?
A question never can be answered.

18. A question never be answered, an answer never be proven satisfactory

Is it really sad when someone dies?
All the seconds the pain they get isn't equal to death
All those happy memories... those moments aren't death itself
Maybe not?
I lost someone to death,
I miss him but I'm happy for him finally finding peace
He is resting at ease
No matter how much I please
I beg...
He won't come back
It's more like he fell in love with death and death said "yes"
They are together now. Happy.

The soul leaves

But do you really think it doesn't grieves?
The soul doesn't sees the pain in our eyes?
Souls are pure, kind, beautiful they give the body
abilities to breathe. To function
All good and bad things are done by body
After all those seconds staying with the body it leaves
like nothing? Why?

I question myself
Why did he leave
He didn't even waited for last goodbye
Or he did?
 I just failed it.
I regret.
He is in a better place now rather than being surrounded
by people who he was
Soul always is in search of a body
To hold it Together.
Still it left like that?
Funny how we blame bodies for letting the other bodies
go in a blink
When souls do the same
Am I gaslighting myself by this last two lines maybe?
Anyways "all the people, all the lovers, all the friends i
hope they all get their happy end in the end<3" (conan
gray)

(To those unspoken words those non-answerable
questions to those all people who makes sky more
prettier and moon less to not at all lonely)

19. Moving on

(A painful yet the most beautiful phase)

Those sound of rain "tip tip tip"
Now feels better than his voice
That laugh with friends and going to that one place is
more peaceful than just seeing him on the screen while
he priortises his games
Those tears of pain
Of not having him gives more happiness he could ever
give to me
Those moments I spent with flowers and cats and myself
is the time I want to stop in forever
I finally understand the 'why?'
It's because no matter how beautiful his eyes are
No matter how his voice is the only song I ever wanted
to hear
He and me are not meant to be
A beautiful chapter of my life which turned into the
most heartbreaking ending of a book
Nonetheless no matter how much I feel the need of him
being here I know I'm better off myself
Those daily fights
Those moments where his friends bashed me and he was

quiet
Those times where I fought my own parents for him and
he still wasn't there
Everything was painful
And now he's gone
I finally feel free
Finally out of his rules far from his friends who spread
rumours about me
Everything is peaceful now
He was a storm which tore me apart yet I enjoyed
But now it's over spring came again and sun shines
brighter than ever and all I wish is
All my lovers all my friends all the people I hope they
get their happy end with them or without but a happy
end

20. I fell in love

Those lavender scented candles
The way they handled me
I fell in love again

The way they kissed...
And the letters they wrote when they miss
I fell in love again

That one condition of giving love unconditional
And them saying yes to it
I fell in love again

Those unsaid millions of I love you's
And
Those laughs when I see the amuse you

I fell in love a million times
I fell in love with every step you took
Every kiss you gave
Every hi's you said
Every good morning every good night
I fell in love again

That first love leaving broken hearted thinking I would
never love again

But here's us seeing each other in eyes...
staring at those eyes
I fell in love again

I fell in love with you
I fell in love with love again
I fell in love with hope and the pain
Which brought me down this lane

Thanks to me and those people in which there's an us
and a you who helped me

I fell in love again
I felt the love again

And

I fell in love with everything I have

Thanks to those people where there's you and us
I fell in love with myself

-narrated by love

21. Mess

A mess can never be cleaned
A mess whose smile can never be redeemed
Imperfection is the perfect word for mess
Why can't it be best?
At least in one aspect...
No matter how much mess tries never gets back up until
someone puts it back together
Does it lack the strength or the will to be held back
together
Or does it lack the love, the patience, the support which
can wait for it to be held together own its own..
Mess just needs the person who will love it
Who will own it
Who will say
I'm in love with you standing with you"
Kissing every part of mess and mess allows it
Atleast someone loves me
Holding the mess up together bringing the smiles back
Bringing that sunshine
Mess just needs someone to hold it encourage it show it
the first ray of sun and
Be generous

If there's 'me' in mess then there's is 'us' in dust
Dust makes mess
We are together in it...

(Sometimes mess can be beautiful too)

9 789369 542512